The Pillars *of the*

Bohemian Paradise

SANDSTONE TOWERS IN THE CZECH REPUBLIC

A TRAVEL PHOTO ART BOOK

LAINE CUNNINGHAM

I0082698

The Pillars of the Bohemian Paradise

Sandstone Towers in the Czech Republic

A Travel Photo Art Book

Published by Sun Dogs Creations
Changing the World One Book at a Time
Print ISBN: 9781946732941

Cover Design by Angel Leya

Copyright © 2019 Laine Cunningham

All rights reserved. No part of this book may be reproduced in any form or by any means, electronic, mechanical, digital, photocopying or recording, except for the inclusion in a review, without permission in writing from the publisher.

THE TRAVEL PHOTO ART SERIES

Bikes of Berlin
Necropolises of New Orleans I & II
Ruins of Rome I & II
Ancients of Assisi I & II
Panoramas of Portugal
Nuances of New York
Glimpses of Germany
Impressions of Italy
Altitudes of the Alps
Knights Through the Ages
Coast of California
Utopia of the Unicorn
Flourishes of France
Portraits of Paris
Tableaus of Tbilisi
Grandeur in the Republic of Georgia
Paragons of Prague
Hidden Prague
Lidice Lives
Along the Via Appia
The Pillars of the Bohemian Paradise

CONGRESS

MIRKWOOD

STONE NATION

RODIN

SHAI-HULUD

EUPHRATES

STRAITS OF ODYSSEUS

HERO'S JOURNEY

PERSIST

RELAXED

SPEAR BEARER

FISH N CHIPS

ENIGMA

DAPHNE'S RETREAT

BLOBFISH

BIRTH

KINGPINS

GAUNTLET

HORSEHEAD

MARKETPLACE

KATA TJUTA

LEVITATION

PERSEPHONE'S GATE

SHAWL

TANGO

PHARAOHS

SHIPWRIGHT

WEEPING

MOOSLEUTE

BALE

WIZARD

STRIPPED

STREETLAMP

SHIMMER

POD

EXTRAVAGANZA

REMEMBER ME

About the Author

Laine Cunningham leads readers around the world. *The Family Made of Dust* is set in the Australian Outback, while *Reparation* is a novel of the American Great Plains. Her travel memoir *Woman Alone* appeals to fans of *Wild* and *Eat Pray Love*.

Novels by Laine Cunningham

The Family Made of Dust

Beloved

Reparation

Other Books by Laine Cunningham

Woman Alone: A Six-Month Journey Through the Australian Outback

On the Wallaby Track

Seven Sisters: Spiritual Messages from Aboriginal Australia

Writing While Female or Black or Gay

The Zen of Travel
The Zen of Gardening
Zen in the Stable
The Zen of Chocolate
The Zen of Dogs

Bikes of Berlin
Necropolises of New Orleans I & II
Ruins of Rome I & II
Ancients of Assisi I & II
Panoramas of Portugal
Nuances of New York
Glimpses of Germany
Impressions of Italy
Altitudes of the Alps
Knights Through the Ages
Coast of California
Utopia of the Unicorn
Flourishes of France
Portraits of Paris
Tableaus of Tbilisi
Grandeur in the Republic of Georgia
Paragons of Prague
Hidden Prague
Lidice Lives
Along the Via Appia
The Pillars of the Bohemian Paradise

The Wisdom of Puppies
The Wisdom of Babies
The Wisdom of Weddings

The Beautiful Book of Questions
The Beautiful Book for Dream Seekers
The Beautiful Book for Rebels
The Beautiful Book for Women
The Beautiful Book for Lovers

www.ingramcontent.com/pod-product-compliance
Lightning Source LLC
Chambersburg PA
CBHW051249020426
42333CB00025B/3135